D1829308

Where Do Birds Live?

Betsey Chessen

Scholastic Ltd

Design: MKR Design, Inc.

Photo Research: Barbara Scott

Endnotes: Susan Russell

Photographs: Cover: Darrell Gulin/DRK Photo; p. 1: Harry Haralambou/Peter Arnold; p. 2: Fred Babendam/Peter Arnold; p. 3: Tom Bledsoe/DRK Photo; p. 4: C.C. Lockwood/DRK Photo; p. 5: Tom & Pat Leeson/DRK Photo; p. 6: Robert Lankinen/The Wildlife Collection; p. 7: Gary Schultz/The Wildlife Collection; p. 8: Michael Husar/DRK Photo; p. 9: Darrell Gulin/DRK Photo; p. 10: Alan G. Nelson/Animals, Animals; p. 11: Stephen Dalton/Photo Researchers; p. 12: R. Van Nostrand/Photo Researchers, Inc.

British Library Cataloguing-in-Publication Data. A catalogue record for this book is available from the British Library.

ISBN 0-439-01945-1

Printed by Lynx Dpm, Chalgrove.

2 3 4 5 6 7 8 9 0 3 4 5 6 7 8 9 0

Where do birds live?

Birds live by the sea.

Birds live in the desert.

Birds live in the city.

Birds live in the mountains.

Birds live on the beach.

Birds live on the rocks.

Birds live in the marsh.

Birds live on a pond.

Birds live in the woods.

Birds live in a barn.

Birds live everywhere!

Where Do Birds Live?

Birds live all around us! They are in trees, parks, gardens, on buildings, rocks and ledges! No matter where you may be, chances are, a bird is living close by.

House sparrows (page 1) are well named because they nest in bird houses and near people's houses too! Their nests are an untidy mess of grass and other materials, sometimes "borrowed" from the people they are neighbours with.

Herring gulls (page 2) live in coastal towns, harbours and rubbish dumps. Although they are almost always seen circling for food in the air or scavenging for food on the shore, they nest on dunes, cliffs and buildings.

Red-tailed hawks (page 3) make their home in nests high in trees or even in a cactus. Being open-country birds of prey, these hawks prefer large open areas like semi-deserts, with scattered trees and sprawling prairies.

Rock doves (page 4), more commonly known as pigeons, can be found in many cities throughout the world. They visit and look for food in streets, parks and window sills. Their scanty nests, made of twigs and feathers, can be found on rock or building ledges.

Golden eagles (page 5) build their large nests of sticks, with a soft, fine lining, on cliffs or high trees. They live and hunt in mountains, grasslands, tundra, savannah and rocky plains and cliffs.

Like a tiny windup toy, the sanderling (page 6) scurries up and down the beach chasing waves in search of leftover food the sea might turn up. It lives on the coast most of the year and nests in a hollow in the ground.

The horned puffin (page 7) is found only in the Northern Pacific. It flies high over water and also swims and dives in the sea. It makes its nest on rocky cliffs, boulders and steep slopes.

The great blue heron (page 8) lives in both fresh- and saltwater habitats. It hunts in water, marshes and on dry land. It nests in a shallow landing of sticks usually amidst a group of trees or bushes.

It's difficult to think of mallard ducks (page 9) as wild ducks, because they are so common and not too bothered by the presence of people near them. They stay in inland waters like ponds and lakes and nest in hollows hidden in the grass or weeds.

The great horned owl (page 10) can be found in many different habitats, from rocky desert to coniferous forest. It usually uses the old nest of another large bird of prey in a tree or on a cliff.

The swallow (page 11) looks for small cosy corners to build its nest in. The bowl-shaped nests of mud, sticks and hay can often be found nestled in caves, buildings and barns.

As we see by the birds nesting on a sign that reads "Bird" (page 12), birds live everywhere!